Then & Now

JARROW

Launch of HMS *York* at Palmer's shipyard Jarrow, by Her Royal Highness the Duchess of York in July 1928.

Then & Now
JARROW

COMPILED BY PAUL PERRY

TEMPUS

First published 1999
Copyright © Paul Perry, 1999

Tempus Publishing Limited
The Mill, Brimscombe Port,
Stroud, Gloucestershire, GL5 2QG

ISBN 0 7524 1588 3

Typesetting and origination by
Tempus Publishing Limited
Printed in Great Britain by
Midway Clark Printing, Wiltshire

The Drewett Playing Fields were donated to the people of Jarrow in 1912 by Alfred Chaytor, in memory of his late uncle Drewett Ormonde Drewett.

CONTENTS

ACKNOWLEDGEMENTS

I would like to express my sincere thanks to the following people for their assistance and the co-operation they offered me during the compilation of this book: John Southern, Paul Rea, Franco and Allesandra Soave, Jean Fairley, Paul Treanor, Harvey Straker, Veronica Rafferty, David Hodson, Bill Cowie, Evelyn Long, Ken and Alan Grieves, Allen Gregory, Michael Perf, Tiffany Reed, and my wife and family; Kelly, Anthony and Angela.

Special thanks to the people of Jarrow for their continued encouragement and support.

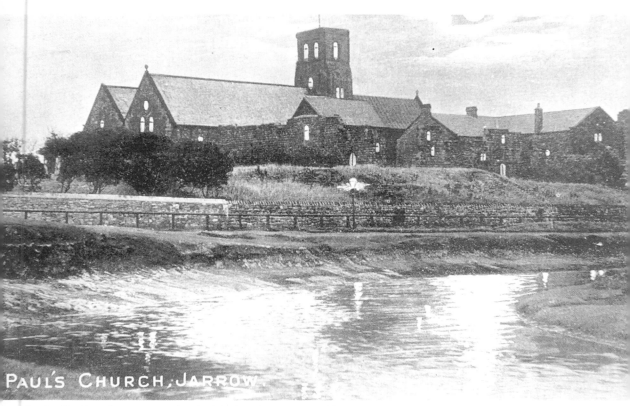

St Paul's church, Jarrow. This holds the distinction of being one of the oldest buildings in the country, dating from AD 681.

INTRODUCTION

The history of Jarrow goes back a very long way. So far in fact, that knowledge of its humble beginnings is somewhat fragmentary and seems to have disappeared during the passage of time. It was AD 81 when, it is thought, the Roman, Agricola, erected a station on the site we know today as the old monastery. It is believed that stones from the disused station were utilised in the construction of the seventh-century monastery through the discovery of Roman inscriptions, found at the site during renovations on St Paul's church in the eighteenth century.

The study of architecture is, and has been for centuries, a fascinating subject – ever since the time man learned to join two building blocks. Alas, not everything today would merit an award for its scintillating beauty. It was the swinging sixties which must certainly take the blame for the many hundreds of troublesome, ugly flat-roofed buildings which mushroomed from the ground virtually overnight. Who was to blame for creating the monstrosities they christened shopping centres? Our towns were robbed of fine buildings of character in order to make way for what can only be described as an architectural nightmare. Not only did we have to shop in this confused mixture of buildings, but we were also expected to send our children to be educated in these prefabricated boxes the authorities called modern classrooms.

When one observes some of today's architecture, it seems that very little thought went into planning. Jarrow, like many other towns the length and breadth of the country, fell victim to the changes, and was stripped of its character. We are all well aware of the fact that progress must be made, and parts of the town must be repaired or replaced as necessary. Admittedly, some of the Victorian accommodation in central Jarrow was beyond repair, and demolition was the only solution. However, when the bulldozers arrived, not only did they demolish these substandard houses, but everything standing in their wake. During this eventful period, many fine churches were rendered useless in the eyes of the planning department. St Johns at the foot of St Johns terrace, the Presbyterian church in Ellison Street and the Congregational church in Sheldon Street were all to disappear, without so much as an utterance of the word 'preservation'.

Thankfully, the buildings in Jarrow that the wandering squads of demolition men overlooked have been preserved, and should survive intact well into the twenty-first century. The town hall was described by the accomplished architectural historian and critic, the late Nicklaus Pevsner as a 'vulgar Edwardian baroque building'. Indeed, some may see it this way, but like it or loathe it, these former corridors of power have retained all their charm and character since they were erected in 1902. The beautiful oak panelled stairway is as good an example as you will see anywhere, as are the magnificent first floor stained-glass windows.

Jarrow has witnessed many changes over the last 100 or so years, no longer do we build or repair ships, and the steel works are no more. We no longer have a Lord Mayor, since the Borough of Jarrow was amalgamated with the Boldons, Hebburn and South Shields, to form the Metropolitan Borough of South Tyneside in 1974. These changes were dramatic, and could neither have been avoided nor gone unnoticed. Similarly, changes occur in Jarrow daily, some so small and insignificant, they are barely noticeable. 'Before and after' photography is the perfect medium to record these often minute changes to our highways and byways, many of which will become evident to you as you peruse the fascinating images within this book. The photographs will portray the town as it was, and as it is today, and with them, the drama of the changing face of Jarrow will unfold right before your eyes.

Paul Perry, 1999

The West Park was a gift to the town by Sir Walter and Lady James, in 1876. The fountain was donated by Mayor of Jarrow, Thomas Sheldon, in the same year and was erected at the park's main entrance.

There are many fine examples of mock Tudor buildings around the country, though Jarrow itself has only a few. Carefully executed, mock-Tudor façades can look as authentic as the real thing, but futile attempts, sadly, look quite grotesque and are eye catching for all the wrong reasons. This handsome Tudor style terrace in Ellison Street has survived the elements, and looks as good today as it did when built around 100 years ago. The original timbers and window frames, have been carefully preserved and should survive well into the twenty-first century. Thankfully the property developers have resisted temptation to change the fascia, to bring it into line with the 1960s buildings of

the shopping centre on the opposite side of the street. A study of the scene today, would reveal the only major changes as being the removal of the Victorian gas lamp and the telephone box, and the inclusion of a pelican crossing.

With the exception of the traffic restrictions, the foot of Ellison Street remains largely unchanged. William Dunn & Co., wholesale and retail tobacconists, were the proprietors of Ellison House, to the left of the 1956 photograph above. During the 1980s, this building was converted into a Chinese restaurant. When this photograph was taken, the shopping centre was under construction, but baker and confectioner Carrick's was the only company attracted to the precincts. Shephards of Gateshead, department store, traded here for many years, until merging with Joplings of Sunderland; only then did they take property in the Viking Precinct. Comet, the electrical giant took over the disused department store, until out of town shopping on retail parks became fashionable during the '80s, when they moved to larger premises north of the River Tyne. Today the property is occupied by the department of employment as a job centre.

It was during the early 1970s that the traffic signals in Albert Road were relocated to their present position at the junction of Hill Street and Park Road. Prior to this they were situated two hundred yards east, at the junction of Bede Burn Road. This move enabled the authorities to prohibit the movement of traffic further down Albert Road, and re-route the heavy flow of traffic across the newly appointed Humbert Street flyover. The lower photograph, by Joseph Connacher a local photographer, dates from 1953 and formed part of a series of picture postcards. As the upper photograph illustrates, the traffic signals, together with the flyover – just out of shot – ensure the constant movement of traffic, and consequently fewer hold-ups. The former Jarrow & Hebburn Co-op offices, in the centre, were erected in

1923. At the demise of the Jarrow & Hebburn Co-op movement, in the 1970s, the building was utilised as St Bedes Parish centre. In 1998 the building was once again refurbished and reverted back to its original use, as offices.

Bede Burn Road Jarrow.

Jarrow has changed significantly during the twentieth century, so much so that parts of the town are barely recognisable today. This part of Bede Burn Road seems to have escaped major changes, if the two identical views on this page are anything to go by, taken almost 100 years apart. Notice the two church spires to the right of the upper photograph, the smaller of the two was that of the Congregational church in Station Street, which was consecrated on 1 May 1871, built at a cost of £1,600 and demolished during the eventful '60s, making way for further town planning. The larger spire is that of The Presbyterian church in Ellison Street, which dominated the skyline for almost 100 years from the time it was built, in 1865. It was around 1970 when the town council, in its wisdom and to the displeasure of the residents in the locality, decided to introduce a one-way system along Surrey Street and part of Kent Street, visible to the left of the modern view below. The the system eased congestion considerably in this part of town. So much so that the system remains in use today.

In past times, York Avenue was a major roadway, carrying traffic to Jarrow from the Boldon's and beyond, prior to the opening of the extension of the A19, in 1965 – what we refer to today as the tunnel approach road. Traffic has travelled along this tree-lined avenue, on what is thought to be the first dual carriageway in the country, officially opened by HRH The Duchess of York in 1928. The lower photograph, looking in a northerly direction, was taken at its junction with Valley View in 1949. 'Pinch point' road narrowing commenced in 1995, where York Avenue meets Bede Burn Road, in an attempt to combat speeding in this part of town. After its success was monitored, the scheme resumed in November 1998, only this time the 'pinch pointing'

continued at intervals along the length of York Avenue, resulting in the reduction of the dual carriageway to a single lane highway and the creation of parking spaces for residents.

In times gone by this part of Jarrow was as industrious as the main body of the town. It was here that the town's industrial past was conceived. The chemical industry emerged as early as 1845, specializing in the production of sulphur for match heads. Many industries followed over the subsequent years, though the only survivors are specialists in the timber trade and an oil storage depot. It was in 1785 when Simon Temple, whose reputation as an industrial giant stands before him, chose a spot close to here to build a fine residence, which he called Jarrow Hall. It was from this old house that he organized his empire, firstly the business of shipbuilding, and latterly coal mining. As time passed, Jarrow Hall was left unoccupied and lay derelict for many years. It was saved from total dereliction by Jarrow Corporation, who converted it into a museum. Today it forms an annexe to Bedes World visitor centre. The upper view of Church Bank is from around 1910, when it was the main trunk road to and from South Shields, prior to the completion of the modern network of roads linking the Tyne Tunnel.

Post-war plans for Jarrow were destined to change parts of the town greatly. The traffic situation was becoming increasingly difficult, hindered further with the construction of a bus station during the '50s together with the narrow roads in which the buses were expected to manoeuvre. The intervening years were set aside to ease congestion at key points. The carve up of Ellison Street commenced in 1961 at its junction with Grange Road, and underwent further major changes during the formation of a flyover, pictured below. Upon its completion, and the introduction of traffic signals, traffic again began to move freely. The tall building, to the left of the lower photograph, was the Primitive Methodist church in Ellison Street, demolished shortly after the photograph was taken in 1968. The terraced houses adjacent to it are the partially demolished houses in Edgar Street.

At one time, Ellison Street covered an area of approximately one half of a mile, from where it began at its junction with Ormonde Street to the other end of town where it merged with St Johns Terrace, close to Greenbank

Villas. Today it comes to an abrupt halt at Station Street, where the Humbert Street flyover commences. The object of this flyover was to replace the traffic signals at 'Carricks Corner' where Albert Road meets Bede Burn Road, thus ensuring free flowing traffic to and from South Shields and the Tyne Tunnel approach roads. Not one single house remains in this once heavily populated street. Today the upper section of Ellison Street is generally given over to shopping, while the lower is used mainly by the four major banks and offices, much the same as it was in the older of the two photographs, in 1888. Maxwells have traded here in the former Scotts stationery shop for some time; prior to this their business operated from Bede Burn Road.

As the shopping centre slowly rose from the ground, Jarrow Corporation predicted huge crowds travelling into town. Provision had been made for two hundred parking spaces behind the centre – not very many by today's standards but in 1961, at the time of the lower photograph, our streets and roads were not cluttered with vehicles the way they are today. To accommodate the expected influx of traffic, alterations had to be made to some roads in central Jarrow. Grange Road almost doubled in width, while major changes occurred in Monkton Road. Perhaps the most significant change of the era, was the removal of a huge chunk at the junction of Grange Road with Ellison Street. Just how much was removed, can be realised in a glance by looking at the modern equivalent above.

Another interesting view of Bede Burn Road, this time at a point closer to the town centre. Clearly marked in the lower photograph is the 'no entry', which illustrates the previously mentioned one-way traffic system introduced here during the 1970s. The L&N store, to the right of the 1950s photograph above, ceased trading here in the '60s. The building they occupied was found to be structurally insecure and was demolished shortly afterwards; the land it once occupied was planted with shrubs and bushes. On the opposite side of the street, there was a small but varied assortment of shops – enough to satisfy the daily needs of local residents.

When the photograph below was taken in 1939, practically every major street in Jarrow had its own corner shop. Shanahans at the corner of Dee Street and High Street stocked what seemed to be an endless range of goods, everything the occasional shopper required from a newspaper, to a needle and thread. The location of the shop in the centre of one of the town's busiest streets created passing trade – a luxury that most other corner shops managed without. Around 1948, Shanahans shop and the terrace of houses which incorporated it was demolished to be replaced by a smart new block of flats above four retail outlets, Gilhooly's greengrocery, Hanlon's grocers, Albert Jones, butcher

and Shanahans. The upper photograph reveals the block is still intact, though the shops have changed hands once or twice, and now offer different services.

Western Road has always been associated with industry, which isn't surprising considering Palmer's works was situated here for almost eighty years. While neighbouring streets were heavily populated, very few people actually resided in this thoroughfare, as it was given over to shopping and other amenities. There were three public houses within close proximity to one another, the white building to the right of the 1955 photograph, above, was formerly called the Western, today we know it as Palmer's Tavern. The building to the immediate left, was formerly the Queens Head, which also underwent a name change during the '70s to that of the Jarrow Lad, but was demolished in 1996. Directly opposite here is the Rolling Mill public house, purpose-built in Victorian times, that took its name from the steel rolling mills at nearby Palmer's.

Chapter 2
PUBLIC HOUSES

Horse and dray delivering ale to the Turf Hotel in North Street, *c.* 1905.

Tyne Street, close to Curlew Road, ran parallel with the river. The photograph above was taken just after the Second World War and clearly shows the old gasworks in Ferry

Street. The house on the extreme right was owned by James Hunter Carr, a local historian, who earned his living by cultivating mushrooms and selling them on to local shops. The Staith House to the left was one of the town's oldest public houses, dating from around 1875. The best part of this terrace was demolished during the '50s, with the exception of the public house on the opposite corner, the Commercial. One must surely wonder why the town planners left the stone built 'Gaslight', as it is called today, standing. In actual fact it is a grade two listed building, and was very probably a coaching inn dating from around 1790, making it one of the oldest buildings in Jarrow, and most certainly the oldest public house.

Kitty Monro's, or the 'long bar' as the Royal Oak hotel was referred to for many years, was a meeting place for many of the towns adopted Irish immigrants, who came to Jarrow seeking work, and eventually settled here in the early part of the twentieth century. Their labour contributed to the provision of much needed housing for thousands of shipyard workers, in what was a boom town at this time, with no shortage of work. This influx of Irish workers were to regard Jarrow as their new home, and in the subsequent years, their offspring were to enjoy the benefits of what the town had to offer them. The modern comparison, above, looks as if the building has had an extension at some time or another. Careful inspection reveals that actually the only major

change was the removal of the chimney stack on the corner. The obscure shape of the building – again in the modern photograph – is nothing more than the effect of a wide angled lens.

High Street was largely given over to housing. With over 400 dwellings, it was the longest inhabited street in town, up until the 1950s. It began at the junction of Monkton Road and Monkton Terrace, and ended at the Hylton Castle Hotel; beyond this point was Church Bank which included Cuthbert Terrace. Curlew Road, to the left of the two photographs, gave access to an oil terminal, and the Mercantile Dry Dock. The ring road around town severed many highways – a good example is depicted in the modern view – as it wound its way to its final destination, to join the Tyne Tunnel approach road and A19. During the 1940s, an oil terminal was developed in this part of Jarrow, evidence of which can be seen in the 1950s photograph above.

When the lower photograph, of John Rafferty and his family, was taken during the 1920s, at the Staith House in Tyne Street it was expected that 'mine host' would be appropriately dressed in white shirt and tie, with a waistcoat. In present times however, our expectations of the landlord are somewhat different. The emphasis is on comfort and the quality and range of ales the publican can offer, choice of which can be quite daunting in modern times. There can be as many as fifteen draught beers on offer, a wide selection of continental bottled beers and what seems an endless list of cocktails and concoctions to choose from in some establishments. Gone are the days when a 'Snakebite' meant exactly what its name suggests, and a 'Black Russian' was a foreigner. This all seems light years away from what John Rafferty and his like, had to cope with, in the

days when lager was unheard of and the most complex drink on offer was probably a port and lemon. The difference is reflected in the modern picture, with Dave Hodson (left), present landlord of the Golden Lion in Walter Street, familiar to most of us as 'Johnny Ingles'.

The upper photograph is the Alberta club in Albert Road, in 1978. This former residence was built in 1890, complete with stables and servants quarters, for estate agent William George Harris. He resided here until (it is thought) 1923, when the house was purchased by a physician who retired to a smaller property in 1935, the same year as the house underwent the conversion for use as a club, which traded at the premises for forty-four years. As the membership steadily grew, so did the need for larger premises. A site once occupied by Gaudies bakery in Grant Street became available and, after planning permission was granted, building commenced on the new club in 1979. The old club premises were demolished to make way for a residential block, Kingfisher Lodge, pictured. The architects of the block have made some effort to design the building in a similar style to that of its predecessor.

Of the twenty-eight or so public houses in the town centre during the 1920s and '30s, just ten remain today, including the Albion Hotel pictured below. Today we know it as The Jarrow Crusaders, named as a tribute to the men who joined the crusade in 1936. Purpose-built in 1865, it has served ale for more than 130 years and looks set to continue into the next century. When the lower photograph was taken in 1925, the licence was in the safe custody of S. Pattinson, whose name is clearly displayed on a panel above the entrance. This tradition is still practised today although in a somewhat more discreet fashion. A by-law, thought to originate from the Victorian era which is still in force today – though not strictly adhered

to – for the protection of children, is the partial covering of windows of licensed premises, i.e. public houses and turf accountants. In turn, this protected the customers from unwelcome glances.

Another of the town's public houses, this time the remnants of Newcastle Brewery's Prince of Wales, photographed prior to its demolition

in 1955. Its successor was built at Calf Close, around 1961. There were two other public houses within the vicinity of the original, above. Behind the camera was the Golden Fleece in Commercial Road, the other, the Commercial is visible on the right of the photograph above. The modern view, reveals that the Commercial is the last of these hostelries remaining to refresh the people of Jarrow. Sadly however it is no longer called the Commercial, like many before it, it fell victim to the trend of name changing, becoming the Tunnel Tavern during the 1970s and today we know it as the Gaslight.

Of the public houses within the town centre, the Ben Lomond Hotel was by far the grandest establishment of all. The lower view, from the 1930s, is from a time when the Victorian building was used as a residential hotel, which it remained until the 1970s. While the exterior of the building always looked as good as it did when it was first built, the interior suffered through neglect and was in need of serious attention. Local entrepreneur Derek Armstrong, who owned both the County Hotel and the Cavalier Club, rented the building from owners Scottish & Newcastle Breweries. He restored it to a very high standard and renamed it The Viking. By 1995, and many lessees later, this grand old building had once again slipped into a state of disrepair and was deemed a white elephant which no-one wanted. It was

feared that the mighty building was to be razed to the ground, much to the displeasure of Jarrovians. Fortunately, brewing giants Wetherspoons now own the property and have completely refurbished and restored it. They have also restored it to its original name, the Ben Lomond.

This was the site of the Ellison Social Club, or the 'Buffs' as it was commonly called. The name came from the Royal Order of Buffaloes, who used the premises – a house in those days – more than seventy years ago. When the shopping centre was built in the '60s, the fascia of the building was altered to meet the contractor's criteria, to conform to the style of buildings in the immediate vicinity. It remained as such until the premises were vacated in 1984, in favour of a new purpose-built social club, erected 150 metres away. This stylish new club, with a membership close to 1,000, boasts a concert room with seating for 360 patrons, a gentlemen only bar and games room among its facilities. The upper photograph shows the building as it was in 1984. After standing empty for many years, the building today is utilised as an entertainment centre.

A request from shipyard boss, Charles Mark Palmer, for accommodation in the form of an hotel for the many world dignitaries and VIPs who travelled to Jarrow bringing trade with them, and rooms for the nursing staff from his nearby hospital, prompted the construction of the fifteen bedroom North Eastern Hotel and restaurant. Having served its purpose as an hotel up until the 1940s, but no longer enjoying Palmer's custom, the North Eastern ceased trading as a residential establishment, and from that time, until the building was demolished around 1994, traded solely as a public house. Today, as the upper photograph

reveals, the area that this mighty building once covered serves as a car park for a supermarket chain.

The waste land in the foreground of the photograph above – now a school – was occupied by the houses in George Street and Alfred Street, prior to them being demolished during the '50s. This was at approximately the same time as the gasometer in the background was constructed to replace its predecessor in Ferry Street. The building to the left of the upper photograph, from 1947, was eventually demolished during the early '60s, making way for Tyne Tunnel buildings. The building to the right, the Golden Fleece public house was demolished around the same time, in favour of housing. The area between was for many years referred to as the 'pit heap', it assumed this nickname because the spoils from the infamous Alfred Pit were deposited here, almost two centuries ago. Unfortunately the gasometer is a necessary blot on the landscape, on what is otherwise a pleasant place to live.

Chapter 3

NOTABLE

BUILDINGS

The town hall and council chambers were designed by South Shields architect Fred Rennoldson and built in 1902. The clock, however, wasn't erected until 1951, at a cost of £1,000, paid for with the residue of the Surrey Fund.

There are many photographs available of Ormonde Street, as it was in the closing years of the nineteenth century, up until the 1960s, when the original buildings were demolished. There was always activity of some kind or another in this bustling street, being the busiest in town as far as shopping was concerned. The only building to escape the demolition men was the former Burton building, which still survives, and is now a carpet store. The entrance directly in front of it, seen in the older of the two photographs, gave access to the market square which was centred around an old Victorian theatre. The theatre was also demolished in the 1960s. Today the entrance survives, but the market square no longer exists. Currently the site is occupied by houses in what we know today as North Court.

When the lower of these two photographs was taken of Grange Road, as phase one of the Arndale Centre was nearing completion, work was already underway on phase two, which included Viking and Bede precincts. Very little has changed in the thirty-eight year gap between the photograph below and its modern equivalent. The shop fronts are almost identical, with the exception of one or two name changes. It is many years since Hardy's traded in Jarrow, Woolworths, on the other hand, continue to serve the population of the town as they have done for more than half a century, from their current premises and their former store in Ormonde Street. Until recently, Woolworths boasted two entrances, one in Bede Precinct, the other in Grange Road. The latter entrance was

closed to the public in a bid to combat petty crime. In its heyday the centre attracted large crowds, today shoppers much prefer the indoor shopping malls of Eldon Square and the Metro Centre.

Both sides of Grange Road contained a good variety of shops and public houses. The Station Hotel is just visible to the right of the photograph from 1945. To the left of this, adjacent to the town hall, was another – the Alnwick Castle Hotel, on the corner of Walter Street. With the exception of the two buildings to the left of the town hall – namely the Masonic Hall, and Sunderland and South Shields Water Board offices, Grange Road has completely changed. The decaying shops and public houses were demolished, making way for shopping precincts and a housing complex, part of which is visible, towering over and to the right of the town hall, in the modern photograph.

Although the urn at the top of the war memorial differs slightly in these two photographs, the rest of the monument remains exactly as it did when it was presented as a gift to the Corporation by the management of Palmer's Shipbuilding Co. The statue of Sir Charles Mark Palmer was erected in 1904 in the grounds of the hospital he built in Clayton Street and was dedicated to the memory of his first wife, Jane. Towards the end of the 1970s, the statue was relocated to a site overlooking the River Tyne. Today, arrangements are being made to restore the statue to its former glory after acts of vandalism and to reposition it in the town centre. Clayton Street and the old hospital no longer exist, these were demolished in favour of a more modern Palmer Community Hospital, which was completed and officially opened by HRH The Princess Royal in 1987.

Practically every building worthy of mention up and down the country was adorned with a flag pole, a tradition which has carried on, to some extent, into present times. We walk beneath, and on some occasions past them, several times a day without noticing them, at least until they are draped with flags. Even then, interest and a second glance, tend only to be generated when the flags are flying at half-mast. The 1950s view of Grange Road was taken at the junction of Ferry Street, to the right. Although Gray Street – to the left – has disappeared, Ferry Street remains, though not in exactly the same position, it was repositioned to make way for the Market Square housing development in 1963, and is now a continuation of

Staple Road. With the exception of the town hall and Christ Church, Grange Road has changed beyond recognition.

The original Palmer Hospital in Clayton Street was officially opened in 1871 by its founder Charles Mark Palmer, in memory of his late wife Jane, to whom the building was

dedicated. After a life span exceeding 100 years, the ageing hospital had become most uneconomical, and was subsequently demolished in the late 1970s, in favour of a more modern hospital, which was officially opened by The Princess Royal – then HRH Princess Anne – in 1987. In 1984 we see the structure being fitted with roof trusses with, below, the completed building as it looks today. The Palmer Community Hospital, as it is now called, is managed by South Tyneside Area Health Authority and has among its services: in-house chiropody, dentistry departments and a day hospital specialising in the care and needs of the elderly. Christ Church rectory is just visible on the left of both photographs.

The shops at the junction of Wear Street, and Clayton Street, changed hands many times from the end of the nineteenth century, when the block was built. It was demolished in the early '70s, as part of the town's on going post-war improvement programme. The corner site was used as a stationers office, prior to this it was a fruit shop (during the 1920s and '30s). Hidden from view in the lower photograph in 1968, but clearly visible in the modern day equivalent, is a good example of a fine Victorian residence – Christ Church rectory, originally built as a Mission House and as a memorial to its founder, Edward Liddell. An inscription above the door reads, 'A memorial of the many virtues and Christian works of Edward Liddell, sometime rector of Jarrow, and honorary Canon of Durham

Cathedral, and Christina his wife.' A date stone reveals that the house, with its rather unusual and decorative gables, was built in 1884. The Palmer Community Hospital is in the background of the upper photograph in 1999.

The public baths in Walter Street were officially opened by the Lady Mayoress, Mrs C.M. James, in 1911. The population of Jarrow was provided with bathing facilities, a swimming pool and, in the 1930s and '40s, a dance venue and physical training centre during the winter months. By 1982 it was thought that the tired old building had served its purpose and was not worthy of refurbishment, as extensive facilities had become available at Temple Park Leisure Centre at South Shields, and neighbouring Hebburn. Although a full-size swimming pool was one of the attractions, another was the bathing facilities – a luxury which few houses in Jarrow enjoyed when this establishment was erected. As sanitation became one of the council's priorities, conditions rapidly improved with more and more houses being built with facilities. The need for 'slipper baths', as they were termed, decreased sufficiently for the service to be terminated by the mid-1950s. Minor alterations were made to the ageing building in 1970, which included the installation of a sauna bath and a solarium, prior to its demolition in 1984.

It was the partnership of Arnott and Chippendale, who dreamed up the name Arndale and who were probably the first to become involved with inner city 1960s style shopping malls. Consequently, the four-storey white building in the centre of the lower photograph was named Arndale House. The first two floors of the building were utilised as offices, while the upper floors were given over for use as Club Franchi, an exclusive night spot brainchild of a consortium of Italian brothers, Franchi and Valente. Continental style nightclubs were fashionable and appeared in most towns and cities during the '60s, with major stars from the world of entertainment being the main attraction. Meanwhile in nearby South Shields, the

Baily Organisation was gathering strength with a chain of such clubs, the first of which was the Latino.

American style tenpin bowling centres were more popular in the south of the country, but were eventually to drift north by the 1960s. Jarrow was chosen in 1962, as the location for the first of such centres, to be located beneath Arndale House.

The popularity of the pastime grew and leagues were formed as the craze swept the north east, bowling alleys were springing up seemingly overnight. In 1964, the Dogs Bowl was opened in South Shields on the site of the former greyhound stadium, this was followed by Excel bowling centres in Sunderland, Gateshead and Newcastle. By the late '60s, with the game rapidly losing its popularity, the north east was overcrowded with bowling alleys. Jarrow, the first to open, was the first to close – in 1968 after a life span of just six years. The remainder closed in a short space of time, with the exception of Newcastle and Sunderland, which today are enjoying a revival of the game, along with recently opened centres in nearby Washington and the Metro Centre.

Chapter 4
SHOPS AND
BUSINESSES

M anagement and members of staff
of the Forge & Hammer Stores
Ltd, enjoy their picnic on a day trip to
the races in 1900.

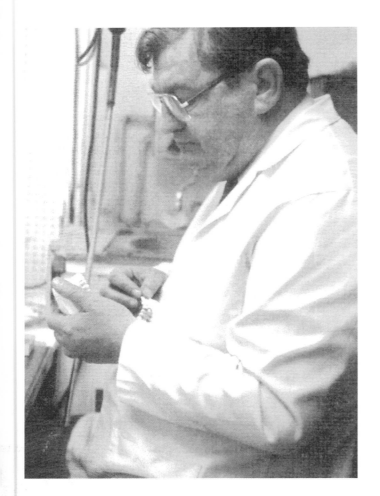

Sunderland. Perhaps it was the misfortune of a broken arm that was responsible for his redundancy in 1967 and the events of the forthcoming years. In 1970, with the assistance of a good friend, Irishman Jimmy Fahy, he opened a dental laboratory in South Shields and after four years transferred the business to Humbert Street, Jarrow as the Jarrow Dental Laboratory. Meanwhile, Eric's son, Paul, was developing an interest in his father's work and after completing his education, followed in his footsteps, commencing his training at Newcastle Dental Hospital and University, learning all aspects of modern dental technology. In 1980, with Eric in semi-retirement and Paul fully qualified and experienced in his profession, premises were purchased in Bede Burn Road in order to carry on the laboratory. Today Paul is continuing the tradition of 'setting up' using an articulator, similar to that used by his father in the photograph above.

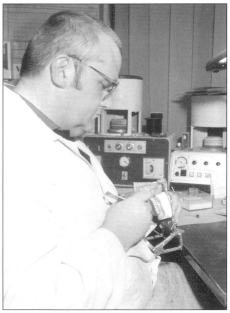

Upon leaving St Aloysius school in 1946, Eric Treanor was encouraged to seek secure employment within the confines of Palmer's offices, which he did. Deep down in his heart, however, he knew this was not the way he wanted to earn his living. In 1947 an opportunity arose for a trainee prosthodontic dental technician at Brabazon's dental surgery in Jarrow, an opportunity Eric couldn't pass by. Three years into his training it was temporarily interrupted by two years national service in the Royal Air Force; he recommenced his training in 1952 and after qualifying, promptly found work in

During the early part of the twentieth century, Jarrow accommodated a moderate influx of Irish immigrant workers, who were attracted to the town and the work it had to offer. Around the same time, though not in such numbers as our Irish cousins, a small number of Italian families were beginning to settle in north-east England. Salvatore Rea and his wife Martha originally came to England from Arpino in southern Italy, arriving in Middlesborough in 1898, where they resided for a period of seven years. After a further year in Newcastle, they decided Jarrow was where they wanted to make their living selling ice cream, which they did for many years. During the 1930s, in what would seem an unlikely combination, while running an ice cream parlour Salvatore, assisted by his eldest son Dominic, busied himself with a demolition business, which he operated from a garage in Pitt Street, pictured below.

In the 1960s he gave up the demolition business to pursue a career in road haulage. Today the business is operated by the late Dominic's eldest son Paul, whose sons, Paul Jnr and Kevin, are directors of the firm Paul Rea Haulage & Co. Ltd, who operate a fleet of twenty trucks from a depot in Curlew Road.

In 1913 Matthew Henry Southern started his timber business at Skinnerburn Road, Newcastle and it was from here he supplied the shipyards, heavy engineering works and collieries in the North East. With his two sons, Harry and Douglas, the business expanded and became a limited company in 1947. Eventually larger premises were sought and in 1963 the company moved to a 3.5 acre site at Jarrow, close to the River Tyne, which was ideal both in size and for sideloader operation. Over the years the company has expanded to 5.5 acres, increasing its numbers of sawmills, storage sheds and timber treatment plants. In 1985 M.H. Southern & Co. Ltd purchased Clayton & Armstrong Ltd, a similar company at Tyne Dock, which was founded in 1800. In 1996 they also acquired Tweedside Timber & Joinery at Berwick-upon-Tweed. Today Douglas remains a director, while Matthew's grandson, John is managing director, and great-grandson James is also a director of the company. With the demise of the shipbuilding and mining industries, M.H. Southern & Co. Ltd, have re-directed their focus – to supply house builders, builders merchants, DIY stores, and joinery manufacturers. The accompanying two photographs show loading by hand, in the 1960s and a sideloader in operation, in the modern equivalent.

In 1926 Charles Gregory, considering the future of his four sons, seized the opportunity of renting retail property in Bede Burn Road. As business improved, the need for larger premises became evident. Shops specialising in pet food followed in Western Road, Humbert Street and Victoria Road East. In 1927, assisted by his son John Francis, Charles purchased a poultry farm, which they sold just after the Second World War, to purchase Monkton Lodge in Springwell Road, which incorporated a market garden and nursery. It was at this point that the market garden was amalgamated with the shops to create the firm of C.W. Gregory Ltd. Eventually the branches were sold and the business was contained under one roof in Ormonde Street, headed by Charles' youngest son,

Eric. In 1961 the business moved to modern premises in Bede Precinct. After Eric's retirement his son Allen took over the helm and continues this business with his wife Anne.

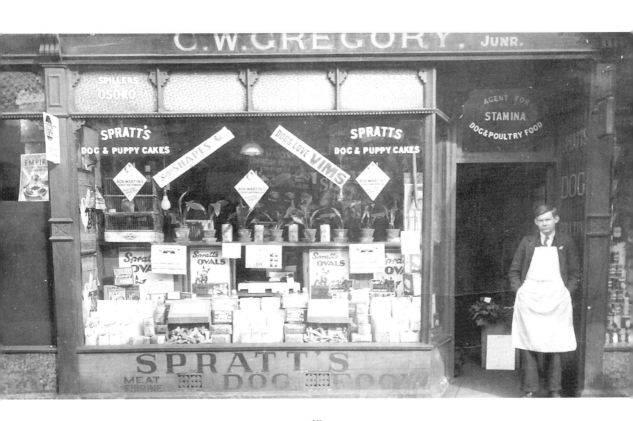

Like most other towns, Jarrow had a good selection of hairdressers for both ladies and gentlemen. One of the most memorable was Joe Chatt in the Market Square. In 1965, while still attending Mayfield girl's school, Jean Fairley occupied her time at weekends as a Saturday girl at Johnson's hair salon in Viking Precinct. Realising that this was forming a career, upon the conclusion of her education she accepted an offer to become a trainee hairdresser at the Carousel hair salon in nearby Hebburn and after completing her training, returned to Jarrow as manageress of the Viking Hair Salon. By 1973 Jean was in a position to purchase the business from owner Jimmy Corn, and she remained firmly established there for the next ten years. The expiry of the lease on the property in Viking Precinct forced Jean to seek premises elsewhere. The Vogue – a salon in Grange Road West – became available in 1983 and realising its potential Jean moved her business there, operating it under the original name of the Viking Hair Salon.

Alessandra Franchitti came to England from her home in Sante Elia Fume Rapido, in Southern Italy, in 1950 and instantly found work with the Italian D'ambrosie family, who were already

established in the region in the motor trade. Quite by chance, Alessandra was introduced to a fellow Italian acquaintance of the family, Alessio Soave who had come to Britain from his home town Belmonte Castello, again in Southern Italy, a year previously, in 1949. He had promptly found employment as a farm labourer, and later with an Italian ice cream vendor and manufacturer in Stirling, Scotland. Alessandra and Alessio married at South Shields in 1955, the same year as they opened a fish and chip shop in Edinburgh Road, on the recently completed South Leam Estate. The above photograph of Alessandra was taken just after a new frying range was installed in 1969, when an enormous portion of fish and chips cost a mere 2s 3d. Today the business is operated by son Franco, assisted by his wife Angela. Pictured below are Franco and his mother Alessandra who, though now retired, still sometimes lends a hand.

During the 1920s and '30s, Jarrow had forty or so butcher shops. Strakers perhaps, is the most memorable, the one most people associate their reminiscences with. It was James Straker who started the business just after the First World War, from rented property in a central location, at the junction of Grange Road and Market Square, which in time became known as Strakers Corner – a popular meeting place for townsfolk. Two more branches opened in the subsequent years, one at Bede Burn Road, the other in Market Square, which traded under the name, The English Meat Shop. During the late '20s James' son, Kingsley, was employed as a butcher at a wholesale meat market in Newcastle, but eventually took up a position in the family business at Jarrow, taking charge on the occasion of his fathers retirement. In 1948, after

service in the armed forces, Kingsley's son, Harvey, joined the business for a period of seven years. At this point in time, 1955, and with just one shop, the business was sold to George Campbell, who retained the name of Strakers until the premises were demolished around 1960.

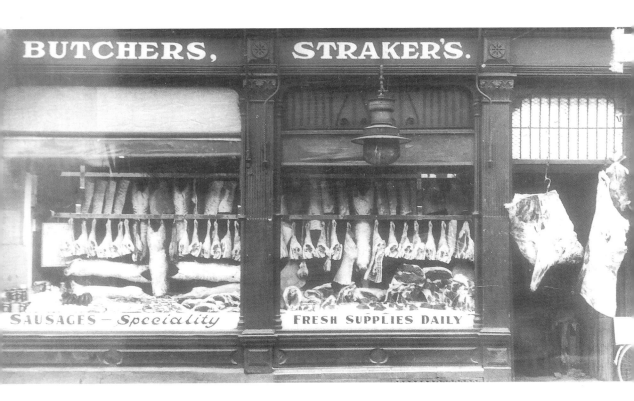

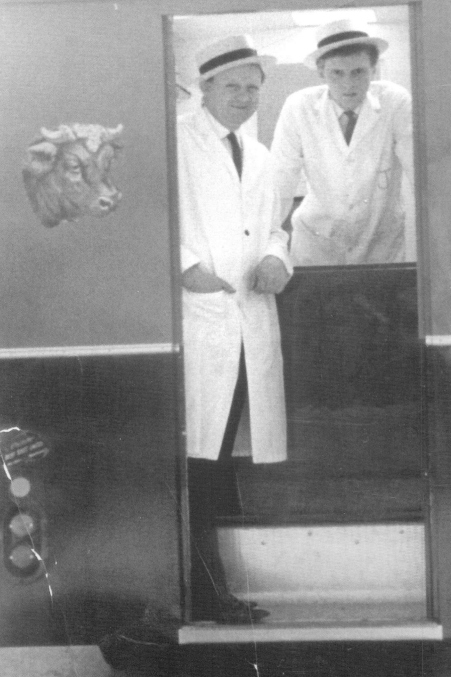

John Thomas Grieves, with his son Jack, established a butchery business in a shop in High Street in 1910. So successful was the business that a further branch in Blackett Street was opened in the same year. At this time best British beef, was priced at 3d per pound. In the subsequent years, Jack broke with family tradition and opened a fried fish shop, leaving his father to manage the butchery business, assisted by his brother Edward. In 1921, after much thought, Edward left the business, but traded under the family name, selling meat through the streets of Jarrow from a horse-drawn cart. By the mid-1930s, he had progressed to a van. From 1943 Edward continued the business from premises in Albert Road, as well as the lucrative door-to-door trade he had built up over the years. Today the business is operated by the late Edward's two sons, Ken and Alan, assisted by Jackson Rowan, who has been with the firm since 1956, first as a delivery boy and progressing to an apprentice butcher in 1958. Presently he is responsible for door-to-door trading from the town's last remaining mobile shop. Sadly this is the last of many which once travelled daily down our streets offering their services during the 1950s and '60s when most shops were a bus ride away. Ken (on the left) and Jackson are pictured in 1967 and 1999.

The first branch of Dinnings chemist shop was opened at a prime site in Monkton Road in February 1948, by pharmacist John Dinning, assisted by his cousin James. A second branch followed in Albert Road in 1952 and two years later a third opened up in Boldon. During the late 1950s, compulsory purchase orders forced the Dinning's to seek alternative premises in Ellison Street, where they traded and dispensed prescriptions for many years. A further branch opened, this time close to a doctors surgery in Bede Burn Road. With both John's and James' retirements imminent, the business was purchased during the '60s by pharmacist, Alan Wilcox, who eventually sold it to the present owner William Cowie, who still trades under the trusted name of J. Dinning Ltd. The surviving branch of the business in Bede Burn Road was vacated in favour of premises adjacent to the recently completed Mayfield Medical Centre in Park Road. The upper photograph, of shop assistant Evelyn Long was taken just after she commenced employment with the company in 1948, with whom she had a long and happy association – right up to the occasion of her retirement in 1996, after forty-eight years service. In 1998, Dinning's celebrated fifty years trading in Jarrow. Evelyn Long is pictured once again below, receiving a bouquet of flowers from pharmacist and former employer William Cowie.

It would be difficult to get one's bearings if this 1957 scene was depicted without a caption, as it bears no resemblance to the scene today. The flattened areas are the remnants of what was once Burns Street, and Gray Street and the car is parked in Cambrian Street. The land lay bare for many years while the council planning department decided what to do with it. Eventually, the post office was relocated here from North Street to a purpose-built unit, constructed on waste ground, seen to the left. During the early part of the '90s the post office was relocated to within the Presto supermarket, until its closure towards the end of 1997. In the spring of 1998, the post office counter service was moved once again to a shop unit in Grange Road and the former premises are now a sorting office.

Chapter 5
SECONDARY
STREETS

The proximity of Walter Street to the River Tyne is evident, with a clear view of the ballast hills on the river bank at the north side at Howdon. These sand hills grew steadily over a long period of time, with the sand used as ballast by empty

cargo vessels returning to the Tyne. The upper photograph was taken in 1950, when Jarrow was entering its recovery years following the effects of the Second World War. Princess Street, and Dunn Street school, suffered serious damage during an air attack, the real targets being the ship repair yards, to either side of the Tyne, and the oil storage tanks, situated close to the river in the east end of the town. Fortunately, the targets were missed otherwise Jarrow would surely have been devastated. The modern photograph below, bears no resemblance whatsoever to the image above. Long gone are the sand hills, the houses and the public swimming baths. All that remains is the Golden Lion public house, just visible at the end of the terraced houses to the left.

After the disappearance of the houses in Caledonian Road, the land on which they stood was to remain untouched for a period of six months, in a bid to comply with current building regulations and as a measure of safety in the event of subsidence. The lower photograph, taken from Chapel Road, shows the rear entrance to the shops and houses in Monkton Road which were due to be demolished shortly after 1957, the date of the picture. O'Connor's grocery shop is just visible beneath the gable. This style of shop was to be replaced with modern self-service supermarkets from the early '60s. The first was Moore's in Bede Precinct, followed by L&N in Grange Road, which changed its name to Fine Fare later in the decade. Jarrow & Hebburn Co-operative, realising the potential of open-plan

shopping swiftly opened a food hall in the recently completed Centenary House. Today Chapel Road is not the thoroughfare it once was, connecting Ellison Street with Monkton Road. Now it serves as an access road to car parks and St Bede's church.

At the time of this photograph, during the 1920s, there were six pharmacists dispensing drugs in Jarrow. Garbutt & Lowe, pictured here on the corner of High Street and Staple Road, was the town's major supplier of pharmaceuticals. Other popular druggists were Messrs Rose and Penman, who incidentally were town councillors. The building to the left of the upper photograph was erected in 1919, for pork butcher Henry J. Abel, who resided on the premises as did his family up until the late '60s. Since then it has changed hands many times, today it serves the town as a fish and chip shop. Sadly, this once bustling part of Jarrow is little more than a short cut to the town centre, as witnessed in the modern view of Staple Road.

It was the well heeled of the town who resided in this once posh area of Jarrow. Most of the elegant old houses in St John's Terrace were home to the medical practitioners who served the people of Jarrow most of their working lives. Dr Laydon operated a surgery from here, as did Dr Sprague and Dr Isabel Forster. The latter two later moved to a larger establishment in Suffolk Street and then on to the purpose-built Mayfield medical centre in Park Road, so called because it was built on the site of the Mayfield girls school after its demolition in the '70s. The telephone exchange was contained within the wall to the left of the lower photograph. In 1955, when this photograph was taken, it was operated by

the GPO. Today the exchange, now fully automated, remains in the same place but is managed by British Telecom.

S taple Road, this time looking in the opposite direction. In the background of the 1954 photograph, above, are the maisonettes on High Street which were built in 1952, around the same time as the Coronation Flats, also in High Street. The building to the left, the school house which marked the entrance to Dunn Street school, is just visible. This area narrowly missed severe damage from an enemy bomb during the Second World War – the school bore the worst of the damage, with neighbouring houses suffering little more than shattered windows. The accompanying modern view, shows that the road was completely resurfaced – this took place in 1966. The land beyond the perimeter wall in the foreground contains two modern schools.

For many years the building to the left of this old photograph of Monkton village was referred to as the White House. Records reveal that it was in fact one of the outbuildings of Monkton Hall Hospital, which was under the care of the North Eastern Association, and which was located directly behind the camera. In the centre is the original Lord Nelson Inn, it wasn't until much later, around 1934, that the building was demolished and rebuilt, in the style that we know it today. The ancient and sleepy village of Monkton must surely have been a place of perfect tranquillity, judging by the older of the two views. Today the village is a busy thoroughfare linking parts of Jarrow to neighbouring Hebburn, and used as a convenient route to South Shields. The White House retains all the charm of yesteryear, after a complete refurbishing programme transformed it into a residential care home. Not quite as grand and ostentatious as its namesake in America, the building is now officially called the White House.

Many of the town's grander houses are situated in Borough Road. One in particular, the former rectory of the parish of St Paul (pictured right), retains all the character it had when the house was built in 1878. This lovely old building once boasted superb examples of interior wood panelling. It has been in private ownership since 1985, but still bears the coat of arms associated with the church and the Latin inscription 'Sanctus Paolos'. Another period residence, also from 1878, which was owned at differing times, by 'several of the towns wealthy', as well as being used as a former police hostel, was Stapleton House. This is now in the hands of Ashbourne Healthcare, who use it as a nursing home. Today, the house is tucked away in a quiet corner of Borough Road, which in all probability is the only thoroughfare in Jarrow which remains almost exactly as it was when built around 120 years ago. The accompanying photographs are from 1949 and 1999.

As a result of the post-war redevelopment program, much of Jarrow was in a transitional state. Plans had been prepared for a shopping centre as early as 1952, all that was required was somewhere to put it. The site where Hibernian Road, Charles Street and Caledonian Road stood seemed to be appropriate, as this was central to all amenities. Row upon row of these tiny cottages – pictured below – were razed to the ground, making way for the shopping complex. Residents were rehoused in out of town housing estates at Primrose. The modern view was taken from more or less the same spot, which is now a car park serving the shopping centre. The taller of the two structures to the right, is the former Arndale House office block and beneath it is the side entrance to what was once a tenpin bowling centre, until the late '60s when the building became a Presto supermarket, which itself closed in 1997.

A classic example of some of Jarrow's tumbledown buildings is evident here in 1950 at the junction of Ormonde Street and Ferry Street. These premises were occupied for many years

by chemist James Dudfield Rose, 'Dr Rose', as he was referred to and affectionately remembered, would concoct in his pharmacy, remedies for a number of minor ailments, upon request. He was responsible for recording everyday life in Jarrow through the lens of his early Victorian plate camera, towards the end of the nineteenth and the beginning of the twentieth centuries. The picture above comes from the camera of James Hunter Carr who, following in Rose's footsteps, recorded images of the town during the 1940s and '50s. The legacy of photographs and information about the townscape that these men left us, is an important historical record, which should be cherished for the enjoyment of future generations.

Cambrian Street, photographed just after the completion of the residential development, Festival Flats, in 1952. To the left are the cold, damp substandard houses of Gray Street and Burns Street. It was around 1956, when the slow demolition of empty properties got under way, that residents from this part of town were rehoused in one of Jarrow's garden suburbs – Calf Close Estate. They were about to enjoy for the first time the benefits of electric light, hot running water and the luxury of indoor bathroom facilities. Jarrow's first local government-run public lending library was situated in Ormonde Street, until a purpose-built unit was erected in Bede Burn Road, during the '50s. Within twenty years the cramped building was deemed too small and larger premises were sought. Premises were found at a

convenient location within the town centre, on derelict land in Cambrian Street, pictured on the left in the modern photograph. The community centre, which came along in 1978, is in the background.

Because of the proximity of the town centre to Palmer's works and the irregularity of the transport system, the majority of the 10,000 workforce resided within the vicinity. The

terraced houses in the above photograph of cobbled Palmer Street are typical of the type of housing available in Jarrow during the first quarter of the twentieth century. Terrace upon terrace of these dimly lit cramped houses were demolished during the 1950s and '60s, to be replaced with more modern dwellings. Hill Street railway bridge, visible in the centre of the accompanying photographs, was responsible for the accidental removal of many a roof from double-decker buses, whose unsuspecting drivers were strangers to the area. Consequently the only bus permitted to pass beneath the bridge was the old single-decker, Gateshead 18, pictured above *en route* to Jarrow bus station.

By the 1940s people were becoming more dependent upon public transport, fleets of buses and destinations were growing daily, with journeys to all parts of north-east England possible. Newcastle and South Shields operated trolley buses – an electric system powered by overhead cables. This was a very clean, swift and economical service, though limited to inner towns and cities. The trolleys were discontinued during the 1950s, in favour of the more modern and versatile motor buses, which were garaged locally at South Shields. The need for more depots became evident as the fleet multiplied. The Jarrow station came along during the 1950s, to a convenient site in the centre of town. By the 1990s a depot of this size was deemed uneconomical as more passengers were using the Metro system.

Consequently it was demolished and the area utilised by a supermarket chain, which incorporates a more streamlined bus terminal.

People have been crossing the Tyne at Jarrow for centuries, by any means available to them. In past times, a 'sculler boat' crossed the river to Willington Quay as and when necessary, with the price ranging between one penny and half a crown, depending on the time of day, or night, and the sobriety of the

'scullerman'. *The Dexter*, Jarrow's first passenger and horse ferry was built by Palmer's and saw service from 1883. The second ferry, *C.M. Palmer,* again built by its namesake, was added to the service the following year, in 1884. In 1921, the ferryboat, *A B Gowan I*, was commissioned to replace these ageing vessels, which were withdrawn in 1923, after fifty years of reliable service. In subsequent years, *A B Gowan II* was introduced, and gave excellent service until the inauguration of the Tyne Tunnel in 1967. The upper photograph of the old floating ferry landing was taken in 1945, today the scene is much different. During the '80s this area was extensively modernised with the introduction of a public pier and walkway. Long gone are the ferries and the landing and with them, sadly, the many hundreds of fine craft, which sailed to and from this formerly very busy waterway.

This was the scene of Jarrow railway station in the 1970s. Radical changes were necessary to streamline the railway industry, with more and more businesses transporting their freight around the country by road, reducing the need for manned stations with ticket offices. Passenger and freight trains operated in and out of the Grant Street station, with the minimum of staff. The freight once handled by the Jarrow depot, was to be distributed direct from Newcastle central station. This transformation was to leave the Jarrow platforms bare of all buildings, with the exception of two simple structures, in which to shelter from the elements in this now passenger only station. The introduction of the Metro rapid transit system changed the appearance of old station yet again, as the modern photograph reveals.

Ship repairing became big business in Jarrow and was one of the towns major industries, as the world's fleets steadily grew. By the late nineteenth century there was high demand for a ship repair yard, close to the mouth of the Tyne specialising in the repair and refit of colliers and cargo boats. In 1885 The Mercantile Dry Dock & Engineering Co. filled this gap and spent almost 100 years repairing and refitting virtually every type

of craft from the waterways of the world. As the business expanded so did the facilities, by 1908 dry dock no. 3 became available, thus shortening the queues of ships awaiting a berth; often lying as many as five deep along the quays. By 1955, as bigger and faster ships were built, the need for a fourth dry dock became evident and by 1960 the monster no. 4 dock was completed. This was fitted with the latest equipment, making it the most comprehensive dry dock on the Tyne, able to accommodate and cope with the biggest craft of the day. From the mid-1960s, the yard changed ownership several times and as ships became more reliable, less and less passed this way, creating a rapid decline in the industry and the closure of the yard in 1981. The two accompanying images speak volumes, the upper shows no. 4 dock after its completion in 1960, the lower – taken from precisely the same viewpoint – is how the scene looks today.

While the storage tanks in east Jarrow were capable of holding stocks of up to 4 million gallons of petroleum spirit and domestic fuel, there were only ever two filling stations in town during the 1950s; Rounthwaites in Edward Street and Jarrow & Hebburn Co-operative Society in Albert Road. Compulsory purchase orders by the council forced the two companies to seek new premises. Frank Rounthwaite moved his operation to a site close to Tyne Dock arches, however, the Co-op's new filling station didn't appear until the mid-60s, it was built close to the site of Rounthwaites old garage. The photograph below was taken shortly after the forecourt building was extended in 1967, when four star fuel was a mere 3s

2d per gallon. As today's modern view illustrates clearly, the station was completely rebuilt when Shell took over the business.

Crossing the humped back bridge in Monkton Terrace up until the 1970s, was somewhat of an ordeal as the pavement came to an abrupt end. Pedestrians could choose either to walk on the road or cross over in order to

join a narrow pavement on the opposite side. This is clearly visible in the top photograph from the '50s. In later years, as vehicular traffic increased, and as horse-drawn traffic was diminishing, a foot bridge was constructed on either side of the road, in the interests of safety. Prior to this the structure remained largely unchanged. The terraced houses at the foot of this thoroughfare were demolished during the '60s and replaced with modern housing – set back off of the road – which we know today as the Epernay Estate, named in honour of the town in France with which Jarrow is twinned. The remainder of the houses on this side of the bridge steadily disappeared, to be replaced with modern dwellings and Nolan Hall, a home for the elderly.

The tram service operated in Jarrow from 1906 to 1929. At this point the motor bus was introduced, though still rather primitive and uncomfortable due to solid rubber tyres. Nevertheless, passengers could travel much further with daily services to Newcastle and South Shields. Charlton's buses, as they were known, in their blue and white livery, chugged around town for many years. As the population grew, so did the need for an up to date transit system. This responsibility was entrusted to the Northern General Transport Company, who introduced a modern fleet of buses. During the '80s the company changed their image and livery and became Go Ahead Northern, a further change of name – to Go Coastline – occurred during the '90s, as Stagecoach (the country's biggest bus operator) came to town.

Railway stations up and down the country had a style of their own, and were instantly recognisable, as were the old water board buildings. The older of these two photographs, was taken from Grant Street, in 1948.

The station building dates from 1872, prior to this the station was in Wylam Street. The draughty Victorian building, complete with flickering gaslights, survived on the Newcastle to South Shields line for close to a century, until it was considered past its best and subsequently demolished in the late '60s. British Rail had an abundance of 'scammel trucks' throughout the country, much the same as the one parked outside the main entrance to the station. These highly efficient and adaptable three wheeled vehicles delivered goods and rail freight around the neighbourhood for many years. Today the scene has completely changed, yet it remains a passenger link for the Metro system.

Plans for a river crossing, solely for the use of vehicular traffic, in the form of a tunnel, had already been drawn up and passed by authorities both north and south of the River Tyne, as part of the post-war road improvement scheme. This was as a result of the neighbouring towns and cities becoming rapidly both congested and polluted, with what seemed an endless convoy of traffic travelling to and from the north. Work commenced on the £8.5 million Tyne Tunnel in 1960 and it was fully operational by 1967, linking with a £3.5 million network of dual carriageways and approach roads, which eventually linked the A1 in Northumberland and the A19 in the south of the region. The construction of the southern approach

road severed a valley at Low Simonside, which caused the removal of the 'white pipe' necessitating the creation of an alternative route for safe disposal of the sewage it carried to the River Don.

In some cases of 'then and now' photography, it is quite difficult to find any significant changes at all. The differences between two photographs, taken perhaps fifty years apart, can often be so minute that they go

unnoticed. The changes in the two photographs illustrated here are so evident you couldn't fail to miss them! In fact the only survivors are the perimeter wall and the wall below the steel bridge spanning the foot of Albert Road, which supported the rails carrying the mineral and passenger trains from Newcastle to South Shields. Today the line is used solely for Metro journeys between South Shields and Newcastle Airport. The opening to the right of the upper photograph, next to the shop, contained the giant steps which were used to gain access to Victor Street. This part of Albert Road no longer exists, the area was completely demolished from Croft Terrace to beyond William Street, for the purpose of creating a housing estate in the late '60s.

Chapter 7

SCHOOLS AND

CHURCHES

The former Government school, latterly Bede Burn, was built in 1873. At this time education wasn't free but Government grants were available to offset the cost borne by parents.

As churches were built in the relevant parishes, church schools began to appear and in many cases were attached to the church itself. St Bedes Roman Catholic school was erected around 1868 to cater for the needs of a rapidly expanding parish.

Initially, the school – originally situated in Chapel Road – only accommodated senior girls, the church governing bodies believing that these girls would provide a pool of monitors and pupil teachers to meet the needs of the growing Roman Catholic community, following an influx of Irish immigrants. In 1870 a new section of the school was built in Monkton Road, pictured above in 1965, which accommodated the juniors, while the cellars of the building provided classrooms for the infants. One can only imagine how cold and damp it must have been for children of such tender years. Today the infants are taught in bright airy classrooms in a modern school in Staple Road, while the juniors are educated in larger premises in Harold Street.

The intricate network of road markings and traffic bollards in the upper photograph, is evidence enough of the amount of traffic that this busy junction, where Wood Terrace meets York Avenue, handles daily. This carve up and narrowing of traffic lanes, in one of Jarrow's most picturesque avenues, has been in operation only in recent years. Prior to this, a simple 'halt' sign seemed to be all that was required, visible in the older of the two photographs, from 1950. Apart from these changes, which were designed to regulate and ensure a smooth flow of traffic, the scene is much the same today. The exception is the addition of St Matthew's church, whose services were performed at Belsfield girls school, nearby, at the formation of the parish in 1935 until the church, as we know it today, was constructed in 1958.

When the houses in Park Road were constructed, towards the end of the nineteenth century, photography was still very much in its infancy. In some early photographs (as above) artists would sketch in details that were not picked up by the camera. This is illustrated by the chimneys of Palmer's works, to the left of the above photograph – one in a series of picture postcards issued around the turn of the century. The building on the extreme right was the Chapel of the Good Shepherd. As illustrated in the modern version, the chapel, which was demolished during the '70s, was replaced with private housing. The rather grand house in the centre is now the local Labour Party headquarters.

The 720 seat Baptist chapel in Clayton street was accessible from both Grange Road and Station Street when it was built in 1879. Today it is surrounded by the buildings of the Palmer Community Hospital. Consequently the chapel now seems tucked away and can only be reached by a lane to the side of the chapel and by Grange Road West. Very little has changed since the lower photograph was taken in 1953, with the exception of the demolition of the houses in McIntyre Street, to the right, and the removal of the smoking chimney. The latter was demolished to conform to local government regulations, with the introduction of a smoke-free zone policy, which also meant an alternative fuel to coal had to be found for both industry and domestic heating. Coke and anthracite were tried, tested and proved to be a very

successful alternative. The white building in the centre of the photograph was the premises of the Tyne Commercial Building Society, looking rather conservative by today's standards of flamboyant building society establishments.

With the exception of the removal of the Longmore memorial drinking fountain and the demolition of the houses behind it, this scene remains almost exactly as it did a century ago. The fountain was relocated to a prime site in Springwell Park in 1921, but no one seems able to recollect what became of the horse trough which stood alongside it. Christ Church, in the centre, was erected and consecrated in 1869. At this time, religion played a major part in the lives of the people of Jarrow. This is evident from the information that at the turn of the century there were no less than twelve churches and chapels, of all denominations within the confines of the town centre, all in close proximity to one another. Today just four of the original twelve remain, the others perhaps victims of dwindling congregations.

As in most towns and cities, streets and buildings were sometimes named in honour of former councillors and eminent citizens. Chaytor Street, pictured here, was named in memory of Alfred Henry Chaytor, a New Zealander who inherited Jarrow Hall from his uncle, Drewett Ormonde Drewett – it is from this man we get the names Ormonde Street and the Drewett Playing Fields. Chaytor Street has changed considerably over the last fifty or so years, today it forms part of the ring road around Jarrow, removing the burden of heavy traffic from the town centre. St Peter's church – illustrated below – was consecrated on 29 June 1881. Originally the 400 seat church boasted a 117 foot spire, but this was demolished during the Second World War by a wandering barrage balloon, which broke free from its

moorings in the gasworks yard, behind the church. All that remains of this part of Jarrow are the terraced houses to the left of the photographs. The land which was taken up by the church and gasworks is now the property of chemical giants Rohm & Haas.

This was the idyllic scene in Monkton village, of the church of the Venerable Bede. The War Memorial, towards the left of the upper photograph, was erected in February 1921 as a fitting and lasting tribute to the casualties of Monkton, who so tragically lost their lives during the First World War. As the years passed the elements stripped the monument bare of the names of those to whom it is dedicated. Members of the Royal British Legion are in the process of refurbishing the sandstone memorial to its former condition. The scene is further enhanced each year with a carpet of springtime daffodils and cherry blossom. The ancient little church maintained its status as a place of worship right up to the 1960s. Sadly, during the '70s the building was abandoned and fell into a state of disrepair, but the voice of local conservationists was heard and the listed building was eventually saved from total destruction, refurbished and converted into a fine residence.

The lower photograph of St Bedes church dates from 1900, and was taken from the foot of Albert Road, where it meets St John's Terrace. The railings to the left of the picture surrounded the Wesleyan church of St John, built in 1870. St Bedes was erected nine years earlier, in 1861, to cater for the needs of the growing Roman Catholic community, courtesy of Father Edmund Kelly who inaugurated the parish. Today's view of the church itself remains very much the same, with the exception of the adjoining St Bedes infant school, which was moved to bright and airy new classrooms in Staple Road in the '70s. The 800 seat St John's church also disappeared from the townscape during the '60s. This part of Albert Road no longer exists, as is clearly shown in the above photograph.

War damage caused many unwelcome alterations to parts of Jarrow. Dunn Street school, pictured above in 1955, suffered serious damage and was all but flattened in an air attack during the Second World War. Local residents rallied unsuccessfully in an attempt to save the school, but their pleas were to fall upon deaf ears, the school was deemed dangerous and beyond repair. It was subsequently demolished, with the exception of one prefabricated building. The authorities – right from day one in 1870, at the introduction of an education act – were in favour of a good sound education for the children of Jarrow. The country's first board school opened in Jarrow in 1872 and was governed by the Hedworth, Monkton, and Jarrow school board, who installed certificated teacher John Witter, as headmaster. Today the scene has changed considerably, the old prefab was demolished during the '60s and replaced with a more modern establishment.

Apart from the road bridges further up the river at Gateshead, the other significant Tyne crossings designed for both traffic and foot passengers were at Jarrow and South Shields. Jarrow's pedestrian ferry service terminated on the opening of the Tyne Tunnel in 1952, although a service for vehicular traffic did continue until the completion of a second tunnel for vehicles in 1967. This photograph of Ferry Street illustrates how dramatically the street has changed in the past fifty years. It was the main access road for both ferry traffic and the many thousands of foot passengers who used the escalators daily, commuting to and from their place of work on the north side. Ferry Street was another victim of the planning department, who

Chapter 8
AROUND THE
TOWN

severed it in favour of the much needed ring road. Today, the Tyne Pedestrian Tunnel is not used nearly as much as it once was, but remains as a valuable crossing.

With the exception of a few terraced cottages opposite where the Regal cinema once stood, Grange Road was largely given over to shopping and other

amenities. The majority of houses were situated in Grange Road West – separated from the main body of Grange Road by Ellison Street. The older of the two photographs was taken on what looks like a miserable wet day, in 1954. Gallons, general dealers (pictured), merged with Duncan Ltd, during the '50s, who were eventually incorporated into the Lipton Group. When this part of Grange Road, close to the junction of Monkton Road and Market Square, was demolished in 1960, some of the small traders found premises elsewhere in town. Pharmacist, George Nurse, continued his business interests in High Street. The corresponding photograph is of smart new houses, erected in 1963 and renovated during the '80s.

Visitors to Jarrow during the 1950s and '60s could quite easily have mistaken the old railway station in Grant Street for a school. The Victorians made a tremendous impact in Jarrow with sturdily built houses and other examples of well designed buildings, most of which are still with us. St Peters school in Ferry Street and the Grange school in Grant Street, although now demolished, were built in a similar style to that of the station. Frank Walke's newsagency, on the corner of Railway Street, served the public for more than thirty years until it changed hands in the '70s and became a tailors shop for a short while. The premises today are utilised by football pools operators as an area office.

Ormonde Street, Jarrow on Tyne

Ormonde Street was one of the town's major thoroughfares and carried the tram service to its terminus in Western Road, a continuation of Ormonde Street. This 1912 view of the street was typical of how it looked, until its shops were demolished in the early 1960s. With the exception of Dunn, Montague Burton, Woolworths and one or two other multiples, the majority of the traders here were single shop businesses, most of which ceased trading when offered modern premises in the newly acquired shopping precincts within the town centre – excessive overheads being a major concern. However, some were attracted and for many years enjoyed the benefits of modern day shopping. Today, as the photograph reveals, Ormonde Street is totally void of shops, with just a few houses. It can no longer be classed as a thoroughfare, as one end of the street was closed to traffic during the 1960s.

Not long after the lower photograph was taken this terrace of substandard business premises in Monkton Road was demolished, along with houses in neighbouring streets. The 10 acre site these houses covered was destined to become a shopping centre, with provision for 100 shops and parking for in excess of 200 cars. Eventually, 7 of the 10 acres were developed and the first units in phase one were occupied by 1961. This phase, opposite the town hall, consisted of 10 small shops. Phases two and three followed and by 1965 the Arndale Centre was complete. In later years the centre was purchased by Town and Cities, a development company, who sadly neglected their investment. The centre was rescued by P&O Properties Ltd during the 1980s, who refurbished it to a very high standard. It is once again a pleasant place to shop.

Not quite an aerial photograph, but nevertheless a good vantage point to record and demonstrate how the townscape has changed in the past thirty years or so. Both of the accompanying photographs were taken from Ellen Court. The first, above, comes from 1967, when the festival flats were still habitable and in reasonable condition. During the early 1970s the former luxury flats, built in 1952, deteriorated after several bouts of vandalism. Eventually the three-storey blocks were demolished in 1982. The 1999 equivalent, from the same viewpoint, shows quite clearly the extent of new buildings in this part of town. From left to right: the community centre, gospel hall, public library and sorting office. In front of these are the recently completed parking and pedestrian areas.

The lower photograph, taken in 1967, again from Ellen Court, shows part of the completed Arndale Centre. In the introduction I wrote of the misery created by flat-roofed buildings, typical of the 1960s. This photograph illustrates the problem perfectly, with pools of rainwater lying dormant on the surface of these relatively new buildings. Most of the water evaporated, the remainder however, eventually seeped through the joints of the protective layers of roofing felt and into the properties below, creating unsightly tide marks on the ceilings. In 1992-93 one side of Viking Precinct, as far as the arcade, was completely demolished and rebuilt at considerable cost to the owners P & O Properties, who seemed to have partially overcome 'flat roof syndrome'. Close inspection of the photograph above reveals

that the 'new' roof is not actually flat, but slightly pitched, enabling residue water to escape via a series of drainage points and disperse through underground drains. Unfortunately the problem persists in other parts of the town centre complex.

Community centres became popular on Tyneside during the 1970s and proved to be a worthwhile contribution to the welfare of our towns and cities. Jarrow CA, to the right of these two photographs, is as popular today as it was when it was officially opened in 1978 by Cllr Don Dixon, Chairman of the Housing Committee, who later became Member of Parliament for Jarrow and is now Lord Dixon. Among the association's attractions are a full programme of indoor sports, squash courts and a 350-seat, fully equipped theatre, which is used enthusiastically by Jarrow Amateur Operatic Society, who produce and perform at least two productions each year. Two more community associations opened in Jarrow in subsequent years, Perth Green and Primrose CA. The partially demolished Festival Flats in Staple Road are pictured above in a photograph from 1982, after a remarkably short life of just thirty years. Upon completion the area was landscaped, creating a pleasant pedestrianized approach to the town centre.